Science to the Rescue

Escape from the Volcano

Can science save your life?

Felicia Law
& Gerry Bailey

Crabtree Publishing Company
www.crabtreebooks.com

Crabtree Publishing Company
www.crabtreebooks.com
1-800-387-7650

PMB 59051, 350 Fifth Ave. 616 Welland Ave.
59th Floor,   St. Catharines, ON
New York, NY 10118   L2M 5V6

Published by Crabtree Publishing in 2016

Author: Felicia Law and Gerry Bailey
Illustrator: Leighton Noyes
Editors: Shirley Duke, Kathy Middleton
Proofreader: Wendy Scavuzzo
Production coordinator and Prepress technician: Tammy McGarr
Print coordinator: Margaret Amy Salter

All rights reserved. No part of this publication may be reproduced, stored in a retrieval system, or transmitted in any form or by any means, electronic, mechanical, photocopy, recording or otherwise, without the prior written permission of the copyright owner.

Copyright © 2015
BrambleKids Ltd.

Printed in Canada/102015/IH20150821

Photographs:
All pictures by Shutterstock unless otherwise stated.

Front cover main image- www.sandatlas.org;
top- Teemu Tretjakov; middle- Bildagentur Zoonar GmbH;
bottom- Ammit Jack
P1- Beboy, P2- wdeon, P3- TybY, Teguh Mujiono
P4- NASA/Carnegie Mellon University/Science Photo Library
P6/7 TyBy, Teguh Mujiono, P7 top- Ammit Jack; bottom- TyBy
P8/9 TyBy, Teguh Mujiono, P8 top a- Fretschi; top b- Valeriy Poltorack; middle a- Bildagentur Zoonar GmbH; middle b- AlejandroLinares Garcia; bottom a- Juancat; bottom b- Ammit Jack
P9 top a- wikimedia.org/Igor Shpilenok; top b- wikimedia.org/Vfp15; middle a- wikimedia.org/Tommaso Cecchi; middle b- wikimedia.org/Eliezg; middle c- wikimedia.org/Krypton; middle d- Byelikova Oksana; middle e- wikimedia.org/ C.G. Newhall; bottom a- Rat007; bottom b- Mirko Thiessen
P10/11- TyBy, Teguh Mujiono, P10- Mopic
P11 top- Naeblys; middle- daulon; bottom- Mopic
P12/13 TyBy, Teguh Mujiono
P12 top- Byelikova Oksana; bottom- servickuz
P13 top- wikimedia.org/M. Hollunder;
middle- CHC3537; bottom- www.sandatlas.org
P14 G.E. Ulrich USGS, P14/15 TyBy, Teguh Mujiono
P17 top- Byelikova Oksana; bottom- TyBy, Teguh Mujiono
P19/20- photovolcanica.com, P21 top- Jet Propulsion Laboratory NASA; middle- NASA; bottom- TyBy, Teguh Mujiono
P22/23 TyBy, Teguh Mujiono, P22- Casper 1774 Studio
P23 top- Kavram; bottom- PRILL, P24/25 -Anton Foltin, Thinkstock; bottom right-Daniel Mayer
P25- Videoworkart, P26/27- Jupiter Images
P26 top- mapichai; bottom- Teemu Tretjakov
P27- IODP, P28/29- Whatafoto, P29- chbaum
P30/31- TyBy, Teguh Mujiono

Library and Archives Canada Cataloguing in Publication

Law, Felicia, author
         Escape from the volcano / Felicia Law, Gerry Bailey.

(Science to the rescue)
Illustrator: Leighton Noyes.
Includes index.
Issued in print and electronic formats.
ISBN 978-0-7787-1675-4 (bound).--
ISBN 978-0-7787-1681-5 (paperback).--
ISBN 978-1-4271-7673-8 (pdf).--ISBN 978-1-4271-7669-1 (html)

         1. Volcanoes--Juvenile literature. 2. Volcanic eruptions--Juvenile literature. I. Bailey, Gerry, 1945-, author II. Noyes, Leighton, illustrator III. Title. IV. Series: Science to the rescue (St. Catharines, Ont.)

QE522.L38 2015   j551.21   C2015-903230-X
                                        C2015-903231-8

Library of Congress Cataloging-in-Publication Data

Law, Felicia, author.
 Escape from the volcano / Felicia Law, Gerry Bailey ; illustrated by Leighton Noyes.
     pages cm. -- (Science to the rescue)
  Includes index.
  ISBN 978-0-7787-1675-4 (reinforced library binding) --
 ISBN 978-0-7787-1681-5 (pbk.) --
 ISBN 978-1-4271-7673-8 (electronic pdf) --
 ISBN 978-1-4271-7669-1 (electronic html)
 1. Volcanoes--Juvenile literature. 2. Volcanic eruptions--Juvenile literature. 3. Survival--Juvenile literature. I. Bailey, Gerry, 1945- author. II. Noyes, Leighton, illustrator. III. Title.

QE522.L38 2015
613.69--dc23

                                                    2015027434

Contents

Joe and Dr. Bea's story	4
What is a volcano?	6
Where are volcanoes found?	
Will it erupt?	8
Shifting Earth	10
Deep below, Along the tectonic plates	11
What comes out?	12
Ring of Fire	14
Mount Vesuvius	16
Krakatoa	17
Pyroclastic eruptions, Hot gas	18
Volcanic robots, Data collectors	20
Fumaroles, geysers, and hot springs	22
A giant volcano	24
Underwater volcanoes	26
Tamu Massif	27
Living near the volcano	28
Glossary	30
Learn more…	31
Index	32

Joe and Dr. Bea's story

Hi! My name is Joe. I have just returned from another adventure with Dr. Bea. It was the hottest yet!

We were on a **volcanology** mission. In case you don't know, volcanology is the scientific study of volcanoes. Scientists like us study volcanoes that have a history of erupting so we can try to **predict**, or know ahead of time, if and when they might erupt again.

To do this, we have to get quite close to the top of the volcano itself. Dr. Bea and I knew this could be dangerous. Fortunately, we had a helping hand from a robot called Dante.

But let's start at the beginning...

Before we started our climb, Dr. Bea wanted to check the **slope** of the volcano. Any change in the slope would be a warning that pressure was building up underground.

She used a special measuring tool called an **extensometer**. This tool has a laser that can measure even the smallest change in distance. As Dr. Bea had suspected, the slope had shifted.

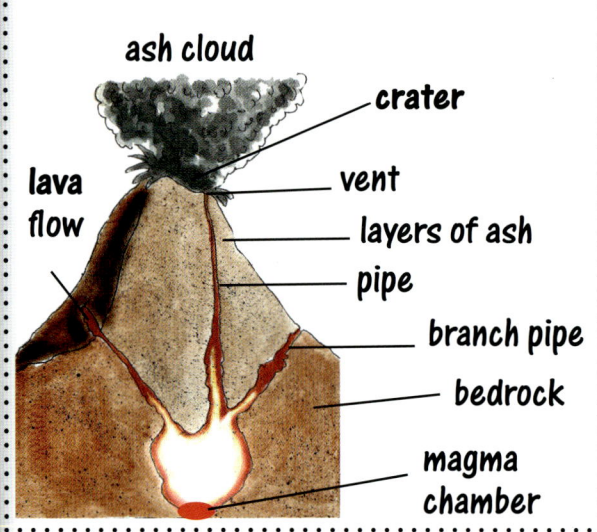

Volcanoes can erupt in different ways:

Ash—a cloud of fine particles of minerals—spews into the air and rains down on the slopes.

A **pyroclastic flow** is a cloud of ash and flames that rushes down the sides of a volcano at a high speed.

A molten lava flow moves more slowly down the slopes, cooling as it goes.

What is a volcano?

A volcano is a kind of mountain that actually builds itself. It is created when rock deep within Earth gets so hot it becomes molten, or turns liquid. Called **magma**, it contains heat and gases that force the liquid rock through cracks in Earth's surface, or vents. When magma erupts it is called **lava**. Once outside, lava cools and becomes a hard, gritty rock. Layer upon layer can build into a cone-shaped mountain. If the lava continues to pour out, it can build into an even higher volcano with a tunnel called a **pipe** running up the center.

Tungurahua Volcano in Ecuador sends an ash cloud into the air.

Shapes of volcanoes

A shield volcano can rise 27,900 feet (8,504 m) high. Its sides are not steep, and its true height may be hidden if its base is underwater on the ocean floor.

A stratovolcano, also called a composite, can rise 8,000 feet (2,438 m) high. Known for their explosive power, some collapse inward creating a massive hole called a **caldera**.

A cinder cone can rise 1,000 feet (305 m) high. It has steep sides and a wide base. A cinder cone usually erupts only once.

Stratovolcanoes can sometimes form lava domes. Slow-moving lava builds up inside in mounds near the top until they explode.

Where are volcanoes found?

There are thousands of volcanoes in the world, but most are extinct, which means they no longer erupt. Around 15,000 volcanoes have erupted in the last 10,000 years, but only about 600 volcanoes are active today. Volcanoes can be created either on dry land or in the oceans.

Mount St. Helens
Active stratovolcano
(Washington, USA)

Hverfell
Crater left by volcanic explosion
(Iceland)

Hot spring (Yellowstone National Park, USA)

Popocatepétl
Active stratovolcano
(Central Mexico)

Will it erupt?

One way to identify a volcano is by how often it erupts.

An ACTIVE volcano is erupting now or has erupted in the last 10,000 years.

A DORMANT volcano is not active but could awaken in the future.

An EXTINCT volcano has not erupted in the past 10,000 years.

Kilauea
Active shield volcano
(Hawaii, USA)

Tungurahua
Active stratovolcano
(Ecuador)

Ilyinsky
Active stratovolcano
(Kamchatka, Russia)

Mount Koryaksky
Active stratovolcano
(Kamchatka, Russia)

Stromboli
Active stratovolcano
(Sicily, Italy)

Matua Island
Active stratovolcano
(Russia)

Mount Sakurajima
Active stratovolcano
(Southwestern Japan)

Krakatoa
Active stratovolcano
(Indonesia)

Mayon
Active stratovolcano
(Luzon, Philippines)

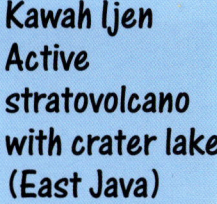

Kawah Ijen
Active stratovolcano with crater lake
(East Java)

Mount Ruapehu
Active stratovolcano
(Northern New Zealand)

9

We both knew the volcano was active. I had been measuring activity in the area for several weeks.

This volcano had been created where two **tectonic plates** meet. These plates are huge areas of land in Earth's crust. When they move, they give off energy called seismic waves. I recorded these waves, or tremors, using a tool called a **seismograph**.

Shifting Earth

Earth is made up of layers. The middle layer, called the mantle, is made of semi-molten rock. The crust is the layer above it. The crust is made up of a number of large pieces of land called tectonic plates. These plates move like rafts across the molten mantle.

Earth's plates are always moving slowly. When the edge of one plate crashes into another plate's edge and the heavier oceanic plate slides under the lighter continental plate and melts into it. New plate edges form at ocean ridges, where lava wells upward.

Seven major plates and several minor plates form Earth's crust.

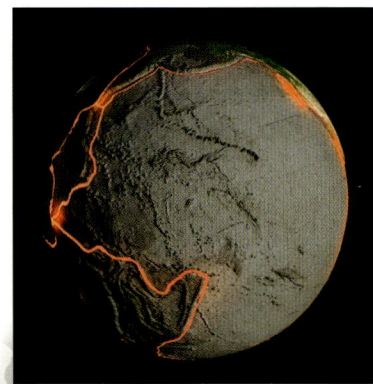

Deep below

Just 25 miles (40 km) below Earth's crust lies a thick layer of molten magma. This magma gives off incredible heat and a lot of gas, and expands under the planet's pressure. Sometimes magma finds a weak place in the crust and expands upward to the surface.

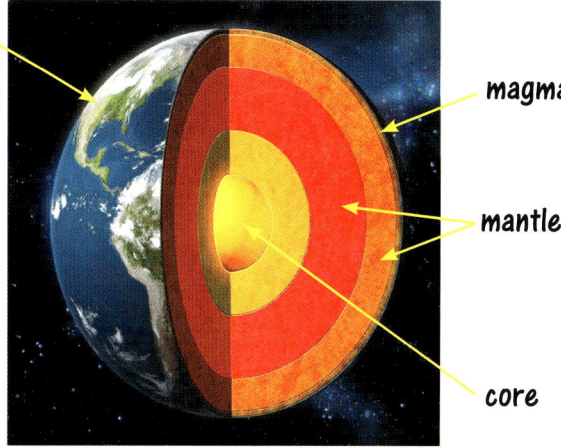

Earth is made up of layers of solid, semi-solid, and liquid material. At its core, or center, it is hotter than the surface of the Sun.

The molten magma rises and forces its way through cracks in the plate.

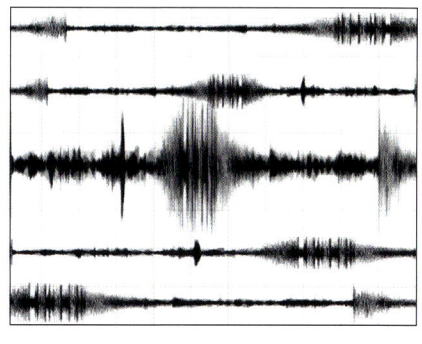

A seismograph is a machine that records tremors far below Earth's surface.

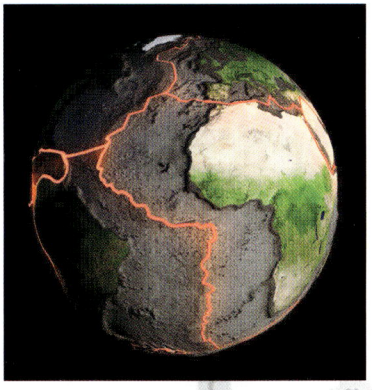

Along the tectonic plates

Volcanoes usually form where Earth's tectonic plates meet. The heavier plate is forced down below the other. Any magma trapped below now has a chance to escape upward, and a volcano is created.

11

Dr. Bea and I made our long climb up to the rim of the crater. It was heavy work. We had brought a lot of equipment with us. We carried an electronic theodolite—an instrument used to measure angles and distances, and an ultraviolet spectrometer to measure the amount of the gas sulphur dioxide. An increase in this gas would be a warning sign that an explosion might be coming.

What comes out?

Different kinds of material spew from a volcano as it erupts.

Clouds of dust and poisonous gases such as sulfur dioxide shoot from any cracks.

When gas gets trapped in the lava, it makes it foamy. The lava cools with the gas bubbles trapped inside, forming a rock known as pumice. It is so light, it will float.

A lahar is a mudflow of pyroclastic materials such as ash, dust, and water. The material can flow down the mountain extremely quickly and destroy everything in its path.

12

A volcanic bomb is a large lump of cooled lava, often shaped like a ball. The force of the eruption can throw these bombs many miles away, making them a serious hazard.

Shield volcanoes can produce huge mounds of **basalt**. This basalt cliff in Taiwan formed from cooled lava.

Very hot, semi-liquid rock known as lava pours from a vent.

Meanwhile, Dr. Bea was starting to chip samples from the rim with her rock hammer. She carefully washed each sample before labeling it and storing it in a bag.

She also had a set of thermometers which she placed around the vent to record the heat being given off.

Dr. Bea collects samples from volcanoes all over the world. **Meteorologists** want to know how much volcanic ash and steam is being released into the atmosphere. She sends her data to weather stations.

The effect of volcanic eruption on weather can be severe. Ash and gases can block out the sun and send temperatures crashing downward. The ash cloud can also change the path of wind systems, and prevent aircraft from flying.

Ring of Fire

A large number of volcanoes can be found in an area of the planet called the Ring of Fire. A string of volcanoes on land, volcanic islands, and volcanic ocean valleys, called trenches, follow the coastlines surrounding the Pacific Ocean. About 75% of the world's dormant and active volcanoes exist in this horseshoe-shaped region.

The Ring of Fire is known for the high number of **earthquakes** and volcanic eruptions that take place in the area.

Pu'u 'O'o is an active volcanic cone on Kilauea, Hawaii.

14

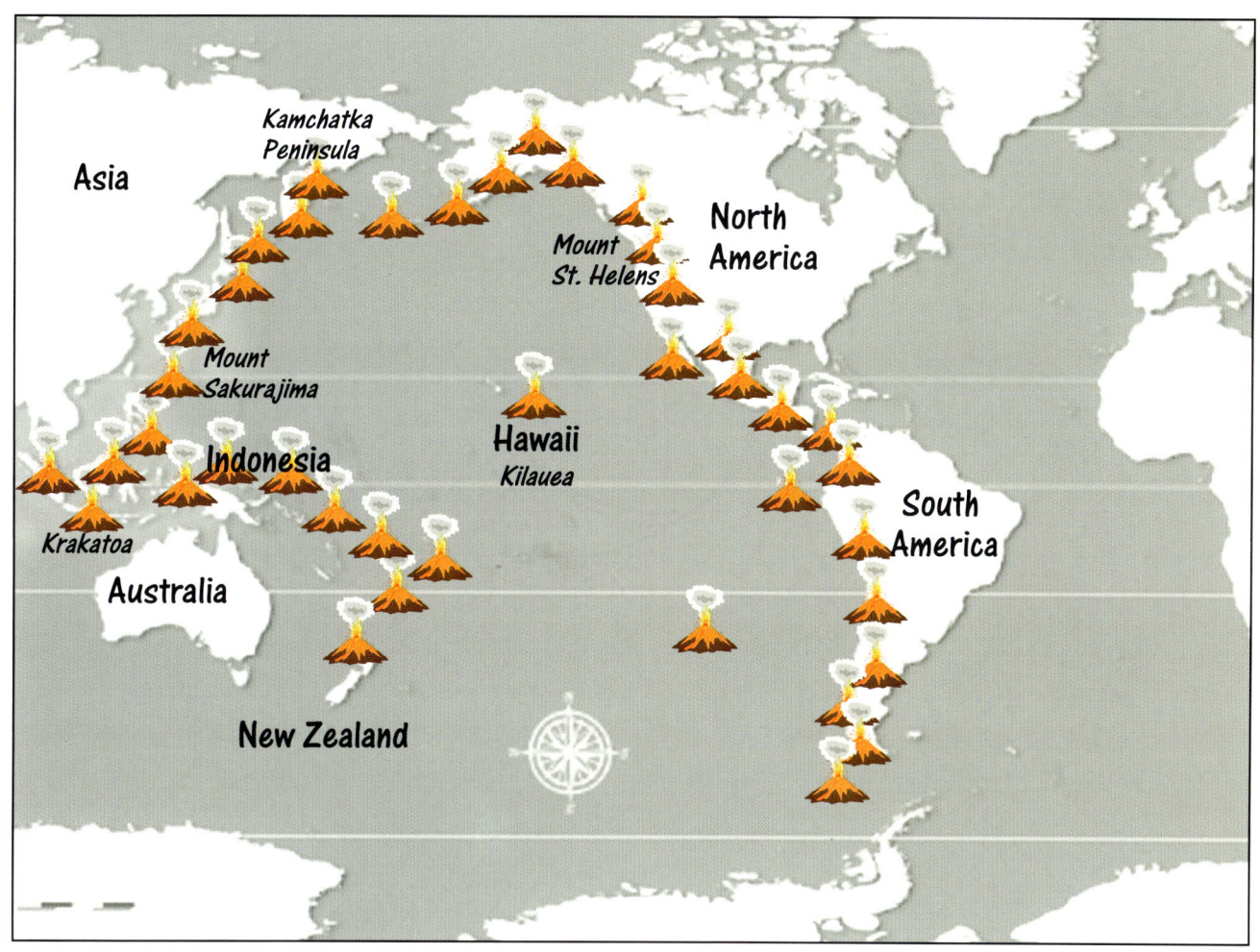

The volcanoes of Indonesia are the most active volcanoes in the Ring of Fire. They are formed due to the movement and collision of three of Earth's tectonic plates, including the Pacific plate underneath the Pacific Ocean. The Hawaiian Islands are made up of volcanoes that began underneath the Pacific Ocean, eventually building up above the water after many eruptions.

There are 452 volcanoes in the Ring of Fire.

Mount Vesuvius

Volcanic eruptions can be devastating. It's not just the volcano that explodes—the surrounding land is destroyed, too.

When Mount Vesuvius, a volcano near Naples, Italy, erupted in 79 CE, the towns of Pompeii and Herculaneum were destroyed. Buried by the ash for centuries, archaeologists eventually found the ruins of the towns. Evidence showed the eruption had taken the people by surprise.

And it could happen again! Scientists know that Mount Vesuvius is overdue for an eruption. Today, about 600,000 people live in the area where people were buried in the 79 CE eruption!

For that reason, the Vesuvius Observatory records seismic activity, gas **emissions**, and other signs of volcanic activity 24 hours a day. They need to quickly warn people of a possible eruption.

Krakatoa

Something similar to the Mount Vesuvius eruption happened less than 150 years ago. Krakatoa is a small volcanic island between the islands of Java and Sumatra in Indonesia.

On a morning in May 1883, the captain of a German warship noticed a cloud of ash 7 miles (11 km) high above the uninhabited island of Krakatoa. It was the first time the volcanic island had erupted in about 200 years. Then, on August 26, a series of huge explosions began one of the largest eruptions in history.

The following day, a huge eruption caused two thirds of the island to collapse into the sea. That started a series of pyroclastic flows that created huge ocean waves, known as tsunamis. When the waves hit the nearby coastlines, thousands of people died and hundreds of coastal communities were destroyed.

Today, Krakatoa continues to erupt. The last eruption took place in 2014.

The red-shaded section of the island completely vanished in the 1883 eruption.

Dr. Bea and I both know that eruptions can happen with very little warning. We wore our protective masks in case of poisonous gas, and stayed alert for warning signs as we explored.

Even so, we were taken by surprise when the ground beneath our feet began to shudder and move. Then hot, choking gas filled the air...

A pyroclastic flow is shown pouring down from the Soufrière Hills volcano on the island of Montserrat in the Caribbean.

Pyroclastic eruptions

Volcanoes can erupt in different ways. Sometimes, instead of going up, the hot mixture of gas and ash flows out of the vent and hugs the ground. These fast-moving, hot mixtures are called pyroclastic flows. They are very dangerous.

A volcano's central vent is shaped like a pipe. Ash and dust rise up out of this vent. However, in a pyroclastic flow, the ash and dust will explode through the side and through branch pipes when pressure builds up.

Hot gas

Because they are mostly gas, pyroclastic flows can move very fast, up to 124 miles (200 km) per hour. And they are hot—sometimes up to 1,112 degrees Fahrenheit (600°C). With that mix of speed and heat, they are the most dangerous kind of explosion that a volcano can produce.

Fortunately, Dante came to our rescue! Dante is a walking robot. It has eight legs that support its frame. The robot is built to be very strong and stable on steep slopes. It doesn't care about the heat—and it doesn't cough!

Dr. Bea and I were able to hold on to it for support, as it hauled us away from the crater and down the slippery slope—to safety!

Volcanic robots

Scientists are often put in danger when they explore a volcano. The ground around the site can be steep and rocky. Loose rocks and ash make it unstable. Scientists are likely to be close to or even inside a volcanic crater. They face risks such as a lava flow, ash spattering out, or a crack suddenly appearing in the ground. Volcanic gases from the crater can also be dangerous to breathe.

VolcanoBot 1 was created at NASA's Jet Propulsion Laboratory. Here, the robot explores a crack that spewed magma on Kilauea volcano in Hawaii.

Data collectors

Roboticists are inventing machines to help scientists do their jobs in a safer way. These robots must be able to get up and down the volcano's steep slopes, get up close to an active volcanic vent, and enter cracks and crevices where humans aren't able to fit. Once inside, these robots must collect samples and record data, and send them back to the scientists who are operating the robots from a safe distance.

The Marsokhod is a robotic vehicle created through a partnership between the United States and Russia. It has been tested in Kilauea.

21

We were relieved to get down the slope and watch the danger pass from a safe distance.

The heat rising from below the surface of Earth can be felt in other spots, too. Water trapped below ground also gets heated by the volcanic magma. As pressure builds up, the gas and water escape and shoot into the air, creating a geyser, or fountain. It can also create a hot spring that bubbles on the surface.

Fumaroles, geysers, and hot springs

A GEYSER is a fountain of hot water and steam found in volcanic areas. Geysers erupt in cycles because the pressure from hot water and gases underground constantly builds up and needs to escape regularly.

HOT SPRINGS are found where there is volcanic activity near the surface. The water is heated by the surrounding rock, which has been heated by the molten material below it. The water is very hot when it emerges.

A FUMAROLE is a small hole in Earth's crust where steam and many other gases escape. The steam comes from water that's heated by magma, but the water boils away before it reaches the surface. Fumaroles are often found in dormant volcanoes.

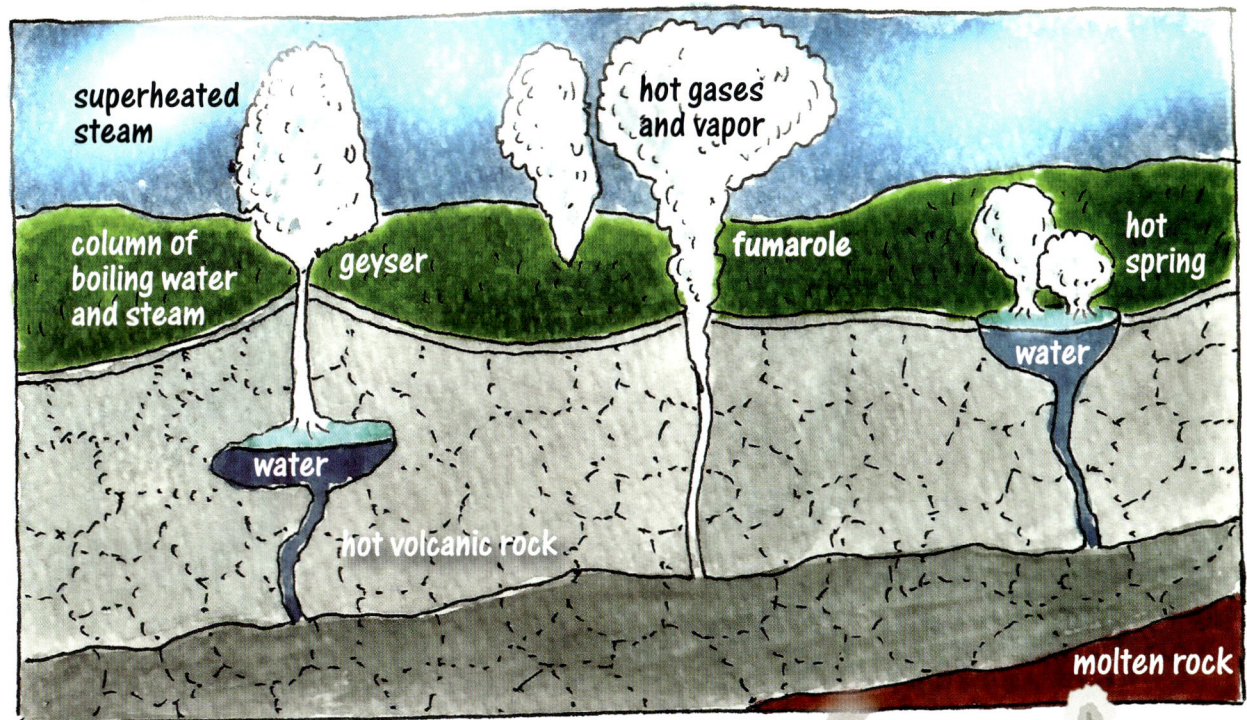

23

A giant volcano

The remains of a huge volcano lie in the middle of Yellowstone National Park in Wyoming. The volcano is in the form of a massive basin, or caldera, that stretches 45 miles (72 km) across.

During winter, bison move near the hot springs for the warmth.

Old Faithful Geyser in Yellowstone National Park erupts every 90 minutes.

24

The Yellowstone volcano, also called a **supervolcano**, began around two million years ago. It began with three cycles of large eruptions of lava and volcanic ash. Then massive pyroclastic flows took place. When the magma chamber under the volcano collapsed, the volcano collapsed in on itself, forming a large caldera. More lava flowed into the caldera, damming waterways and creating lakes. As time passed, magma filled the chamber again, and geysers and hot springs emerged.

Bison have been known to die if they become stuck in unstable ground near a hot spring and can't escape.

Water can hide many secrets. Some of the largest volcanoes in the world are hidden under water.

Dr. Bea and I knew how dangerous these hidden giants could be. Underwater eruptions can cause giant waves called tsunamis. This wall of water rushes across the ocean's surface and can be powerful enough to destroy whatever lies in its path.

Underwater volcanoes

Underwater volcanoes are among the largest on the planet. They may not look tall to us, but they extend deep below the surface of the water to the bottom of the sea.

Water filled this volcanic crater to form a lake in Yellowstone National Park.

Sometimes only the top of an underwater volcano can be seen as an island.

Tamu Massif

The largest volcano in the world lies under the sea. It is 1.2 miles (2 km) below the surface of the water and sits on an underwater plateau in the Pacific Ocean, east of Japan.

The volcano, named Tamu Massif, covers 193,000 square miles (499,868 sq km) which is about the same size as France. It extends 19 miles (31 km) down into Earth's crust. It was formed about 145 million years ago in a massive lava flow. Fortunately, it's unlikely to erupt again!

27

You might think people wouldn't want to live too close to a volcano because of the danger. But they do! That's because volcanic soil is very fertile and good for farming.

When the volcanic event was over, it was time for us to get Dr. Bea's samples back to the lab. We had a dangerous—but exciting—day on the volcano's slopes. But, just like the villagers who reappeared after the danger was gone, it was time for us to return to our work.

Living near the volcano

Mount Merapi is one of the most active volcanoes in Indonesia. People have been farming on its slopes for hundreds of years. Because it erupts so often, the sides of the volcano are covered in ash, creating excellent farmland.

Mount Merapi, which means Fire Mountain, erupts every two or three years, but the last really big eruption was in 2010, when tens of thousands of villagers had to leave their homes. The eruption lasted 16 days with volcanic earthquakes, tremors, avalanches, fast-moving clouds of pyroclastic ash, and lahar floods.

Volcanic soil is good for growing rice, sugar cane, and grapes.

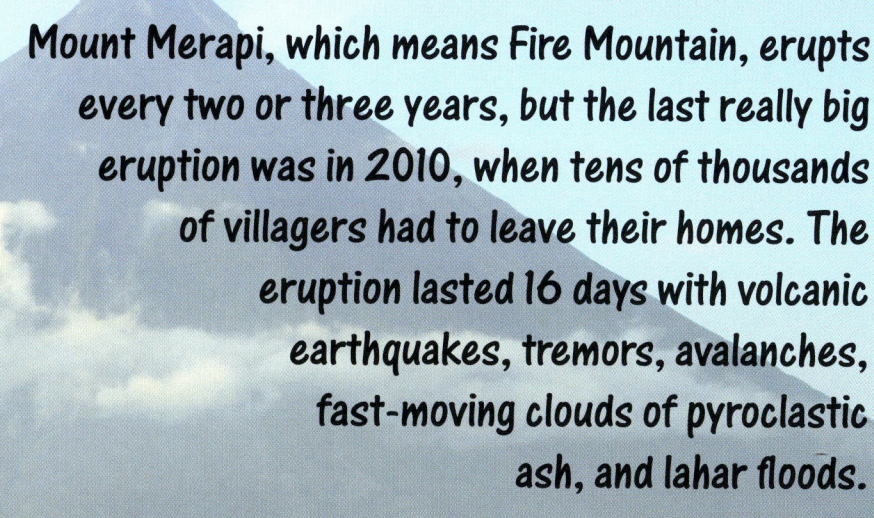

Glossary

basalt
A kind of rock that develops from lava that erupted from a volcano then cooled

caldera
A circular depression in the ground that forms at the center of a volcano, and can be formed by the final erosion of a volcano that then becomes extinct and collapses inward

crater
The name for the mouth of a volcano

earthquake
A large, sudden movement of Earth's surface, or crust, that often creates cracks and breaks

emissions
The discharge of something, such as gases

extensometer
A machine that can measure very small changes occurring in the slope of a hillside

hot spring
Springs that form in areas of volcanic activity, where water comes to Earth's surface at a high temperature

lahar
A flow of volcanic ash, and rock mixed with water to make a deep, fast-moving stream of mud

lava
Molten, or liquid, rock that flows from an erupting volcano

magma
Hot, liquid rock that flows upward inside a volcano, then becomes lava when it is outside the volcano

meteorologist
Someone who studies climate and weather, and can predict weather and storms

pipe
The pipe of a volcano is the tube-like structure leading from the magma chamber to the top of the volcano's vent.

pumice
Light lava rock that will float because of the gases trapped inside bubbles of the lava that can't escape after it cools

pyroclastic flow
A fast-moving cloud of extremely hot ash, flame, and gas that can rush at high speed from the top and the sides of a volcano

seismograph
An instrument that measures how much the ground shakes or vibrates deep below the surface

slope
A slanted surface

supervolcano
A very large volcano which is able to produce huge eruptions that will cause a lot of damage

tectonic plate
A section of Earth's crust that moves as a single piece. Where two or more plates meet, the surface of Earth can bend or crack and a volcano may occur.

Learn more...

Books:

Volcanoes
by Shirley Duke.
Rourke Educational Media, 2015

Volcanoes
by Arthur Gullo.
Cavendish Square Publishing, 2015

Volcanoes
by Peter Murray.
The Child's World, 2015

Websites:

Volcanoes and how they work, with terms explained.
www.weatherwizkids.com/weather-volcano.htm

See where volcanoes are erupting today.
www.volcanodiscovery.com/erupting_volcanoes.html

Information about volcanoes and their locations in the United States.
https://volcanoes.usgs.gov/

Index

active volcanoes 8, 9, 10, 14, 15, 21, 28
aircraft 14
ash 6, 7, 12, 14, 16, 17, 19, 21, 25, 28, 29

basalt 13
bison 24, 25
branch pipes 6, 19
building volcanoes 7, 11, 15, 26

calderas 7, 24, 25
cinder cones 7
collecting data 21
composite volcanoes 7
craters 6, 20, 21, 26
crust 10, 11, 23, 27

Dante robot 5, 20
dormant volcanoes 8, 14, 23

earthquakes 14, 29
Earth's layers 10-11
eruptions 6, 14, 16, 17, 18, 19, 25, 29
explosions 7, 8, 12, 16, 17, 19
extensometer 6
extinct volcanoes 8

farmland 28-29
fumaroles 22, 23

gases 11, 12, 16, 18, 19, 21, 22, 23

geysers 22, 23, 24, 25
giant volcanoes 24-25

Hawaii 8, 14, 15, 21
heat 7, 11, 13, 19, 20, 22, 23
Herculaneum 16
hot springs 8, 22, 23, 25
Hverfell Crater 8

Indonesia 9, 15, 17, 28
Ilyinsky volcano 9

Kamchatka 9, 15
Kawah Ijen volcano 9
Kilauea volcanoes 8, 14, 15, 21
Krakatoa 9, 15, 17

lahars 12, 29
lava 6, 7, 10, 12, 13, 21, 25, 27
living near a volcano 28-29

magma 6, 7, 11, 21, 22, 23, 25
magma chamber 6, 25
Marsokhod robot 21
Matua Island 9
Mayon volcano 9
meteorologists 14
molten lava 6
molten magma 11

molten rock 7, 10, 23
Montserrat 18
Mount Koryaksky 9
Mount Merapi 28
Mount Ruapehu 9
Mount Sakurajima 9, 15
Mount St. Helens 8, 15
Mount Vesuvius 16
mudflows 12

Old Faithful Geyser 24

Pacific Ocean 14, 15, 27
pipes 6, 7, 19
poisonous gases 12, 18
Pompeii 16
Popctepétl volcano 8
pumice 12
Pu'u 'O'o volcano 14
pyroclastic flows 6, 12, 17, 18, 19, 25, 29

Ring of Fire 14, 15
robots 5, 20-21

seismic activity 16
seismic waves 10
seismographs 10, 11
shield volcanoes 7, 8, 13
slopes 6, 20, 21, 28
soil 28-29
Soufrière Hills volcano 18

steam 14, 22, 23
stratovolcanoes 7, 8, 9
Stromboli volcano 9
sulfur dioxide 12
supervolcanoes 24-25

taking measurements 12, 13
Tamu Massif 27
tectonic plates 10, 11, 15
theodolite 12
thermometers 13
tsunamis 17, 26
Tungurahua Volcano 7, 8

ultraviolet spectrometer 12
underwater volcanoes 26-27

vents 7, 13, 19, 21
volcanic bombs 13
volcanic islands 9, 13, 15, 17, 18, 26
VolcanoBot 1 21
volcanology 5
wind systems 14
Yellowstone National Park 8, 24-25, 26

32